Chirpy© Gourmet

Book 3: Chirpy's Magic Apron
Kids Cookbook Series

Robert Bellini

Author, Chef, Food Stylist, Photographer

Kristine Lucco

Illustrator, Friend

Follow Chirpy on Instagram! @chirpygourmet

Chirpy°
Gourmet

Text copyright © 2023 by Robert Bellini

Illustrations copyright © 2023 by Robert Bellini

Dazzelton Publishing 2023

USPTO Trademark Serial # 8869586

IC 009. US 021 023 026 036 038

USPTO Trademark Serial # 88327027

IC 009. US 021 023 026 036 038

ISBN 979-8-9854816-9-3

Robert Bellini - Owner

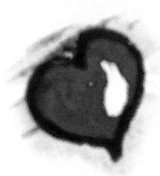

<u>Dedication</u>

To my family, Lucy, and all of the people in the world
who love to read, cook, and spread joy to others.

Introduction

Such fun and exciting 'Tasty Adventures' await you in
'Chirpy's Magic Apron' Kid's Cookbook.

Chirpy's new adventures begin as she finds out her friend Madilena
Pinafore made for her a special apron with magical powers, but it's lost
and Chirpy needs to find it, so she can share its magic with others.

Chirpy helps a friend from school, Curly Unsurely, build confidence by
inviting him to cook with her. One of the Magic Aprons powers,
the gift of sharing, comes to life in this story.

Grandpa decides to test the other powers of the Magic Apron to see if
it can bring him and grandma back to their fav Paris food memory.

Chirpy spends time with her dad having lunch in New Orleans, but how
they get there is the fun part.

<u>Table of Contents</u>

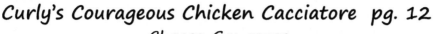

Finding the Magic Apron

Chirpy has many creative and thoughtful friends. One of them is Madilena Pinafore. 'Madi' as everyone calls her, owns a specialty shop in Dazzelton called Madi's Market. Madi's sells locally sourced and produced things like honey and jams, bakery items, pottery, books, kitchen tools, and her own hand sewn kitchen aprons. Madilena recently told Chirpy a secret about the beautiful aprons she makes and sells in Madi's, and other stores. The secret that she shared only with Chirpy is that one of the aprons she made has magic powers.

Madi's grandmother is her hero, she brings joy everywhere she goes, and is a great chef. Grandma made her own aprons with special cloth and thread, and taught Madi how to make these aprons. She recently gave Madi the last of this thread and cloth and it was enough to make one more apron. It turned out to be The Magic Apron. Madi told Chirpy that wearing this apron gives you special powers. Some of those powers are, having total confidence in yourself, the ability to share, and being creative without fear of failure. Having the power to share is an incredible blessing. We all have something great to share. Sharing opens your heart to others and is so rewarding when you do it. You can share so many things, your time, love, friendship, or something you made, like a cake! Madi believes the Magic Apron has many more powers. It may be endless as to what magical things it does for the people who put it on.

The Magic Apron is distinct because it's the only one made with a gold leaf on the inside pocket. Madilena made it for Chirpy, but it was accidentally sent to one of the stores that sells her aprons, along with the other aprons they ordered. "I'm most positive the Magic Apron was sent to Maters and Potaters market on Peach Tree Island. Chirpy you must find it!" Madi pleads.

"Holy Mackerel", Chirpy says, "My cousins live on Peach Tree Island and my mom, and I are going to visit them this week!" "I love Maters and Potaters, it's my favorite organic market on Peach Tree Island. When I get there, I'll look for the magic apron right away." Chirpy wants to get the magic apron so she can share it with others, and they can feel the joy its powers give them. "This is so exciting; I can't wait to get there." says Chirpy.

Peach Tree Island is a beautiful seaside town filled with bustling shops, restaurants and markets. Just past Island Ice Creamery they spot Maters and Potaters. "It's still such a cute little market isn't it mom?" Chirpy says. "It really is Chirp", says her mom. "They support many local farms by selling their fresh veggies and fruit, so it is important to support them." Chirpy agrees. "Just like they sell Madilena's aprons and support her. Let's go in!"

"Look at all of the beautiful fresh fruit and vegetables!" Mom gets as excited as Chirpy when it comes to food. "Yum, the peaches are so ripe." Chirpy says almost tasting them with her eyes as her mom picks out the brightest ones. "Let's make Peach Crostadas with Brown Sugar Butter and Vanilla Ice Cream!" Chirpy's mom has THE flakiest Crostada dough recipe.

The produce section has baskets filled with farm fresh yellow summer squash, zucchini, huge bluish red heirloom tomatoes, and so much more delicious fruit and herbs. Chirpy thinks of her dad's Summer Squash Frittata recipe and decides to make that tomorrow morning for breakfast. A Frittata is an Italian baked omelet made with eggs, vegetables, and lightly topped with your favorite cheese. Chirpy's dad sautés the zucchini and yellow squash until golden brown, then scrambles the eggs, pours the eggs over the squash and bakes it with cheese on top. A perfect summer breakfast.

Chirpy begins the search for Madilena's aprons. "Mom, there they are!" Chirpy points out feeling so hopeful. "There are only six left. Madelena's apron designs are so artistic." Chirpy picks up the first one, "Wow, they are made so well!" She looks in the pocket, no gold leaf. She checks the second one, nothing. She looks through the third apron, getting slightly nervous now because there are only three left. No leaf. Chirpy is thinking the magic apron was already sold. She thinks to herself that even if she doesn't find it, she is still happy for the person who has it, because they will feel the joy that it brings, no matter who wears it. As she inspects the fourth apron, it has no gold leaf. "Oh no mom, maybe we're too late." Then picking up apron number five it feels a little different, and as she finds the pocket it reveals the gold leaf. "There's the gold leaf, inside the pocket like Madelena said!" Chirpy almost screams out with joy. "I found it, the magic apron!" "Mom, it was here! How awesome is this?" "Pretty cool Chirps, you are the keeper of the Magic Apron now." High five kiddo!

As they leave with their fresh peaches, berries, summer squash and tomatoes, Chirpy holds her magic apron. I can't wait to put it on when I make dad's Summer Squash Frittata tomorrow morning. I will share my apron with everyone to bring them the joy of being creative and let them feel the satisfying gratitude of being able to share.

Summer Squash Frittata

Makes 5 - 6 servings. Preheat oven to 350 degrees.

- 1 lg.   Yellow Summer Squash
- 1 lg.   Zucchini Squash
- 4 Tbsp.   Extra Virgin Olive Oil
- 10 ea.   Large Eggs
- 1/2 tsp.   Salt
- 1/4 tsp.   Ground Black Pepper
- 1/4 Cup   Grated Parmesan or Cheddar Cheese
- 2 ea.   Scallions sliced
- 10 inch saute pan, non stick coated preferred.

1. Wash both squash, then slice them into 1/4 inch slices.
2. Wash the scallions then slice into ¼ inch pieces. Set aside.
3. Heat the saute pan over medium heat, add the olive oil.
4. Add the sliced summer squash and zucchini to the pan.
5. Season with ¼ tsp salt and a few sprinkles of pepper.
6. Cook until caramelized and soft but not falling apart, about 8 minutes.
7. While the squash is cooking, crack eggs into mixing bowl, add salt and pepper, and mix with fork until scrambled.
8. Once vegetables are ready, keep pan on the stove and add eggs to pan.
9. Sprinkle scallions then grated cheese over the eggs to cover entire pan.
10. Place in the oven to bake for about 20 - 25 minutes, your Frittata should be firm and cooked throughout before eating.
11. With oven mitts, remove your Frittata from oven. Shake the pan slightly to loosen it. You can slice it in the pan, or slide it whole onto a serving plate, then slice your Frittata.
12. Frittata can be served hot or cold.

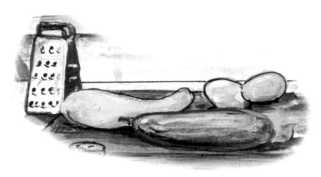

Peach Crostada with Brown Sugar Butter

Crostada Dough and Peach Crostada

Preheat oven to 375 degrees.

- 24 oz.   A.P. Flour
- 3 ½ tsp.   Salt
- 6 oz.   Butter
- 6 ½ oz.   Vegetable Shortening
- 9 oz.   Cold water with ice
- 7 - 8   Fresh ripe Peaches

1. In a large bowl add the flour and salt. Mix together.
2. Add butter and shortening, gently rub into flour to pea sized pieces.
3. Pour ice water without ice into center of flour. Gently mix in from side of bowl to center until a dough is formed. Add a Tbsp more water if dry.
4. On parchment paper, press dough into a square about 1 in. thick. Chill for at least 30 minutes.
5. Divide dough into six pieces, then roll out discs that will be 6 inches in diameter, and ¼ inch thick. Place Crostada discs on baking sheet with parchment paper, about 1 inch apart from each other.
6. Slice peaches into eight slices. Arrange peaches over dough, about 8 slices in each Crostada, leave an inch of dough around edge for crust.
7. Fold edges of dough onto peaches to create a crust.
8. Bake at 375 degrees for 10 minutes, then place a small scoop of the Brown Sugar Butter in middle of each Crostada, Finish baking for 12 min.
9. Serve warm with a big scoop of vanilla ice cream on top.

Brown Sugar Butter

- ¾ Cup   Brown Sugar
- ½ Cup   Butter – room temperature.
- 1 Tbsp.   Vanilla
- 1 tsp.   Salt

1. In a mixing bowl, combine all ingredients and mix together.

Curly's Courageous Chicken Cacciatore

Chirpy's so excited about finding the Magic Apron that Madi made for her. Now her mind is racing with what she can do with it. She wants to let people experience the magic it can create. There are hidden powers in this apron. Chirpy knows for sure it gives you confidence and the ability to share. These are wonderful powers to have. To see the smiles, you can give someone by sharing with them is a fantastic feeling.

I know who I can share my apron with. My friend Curly. He is such a nice boy, Chirpy thinks to herself. He and Chirpy are friends from school. He often seems to be unsure of himself. Some of the mean boys in school call him Curly Unsurely. Thus, he's become very shy and hesitant to be himself because he is afraid of being teased or made fun of. Chirpy knows Curly loves to eat, and his favorite food is Chicken Cacciatore with Broccoli. Chirpy knows this because she talks about food with everyone. Curly loves to watch chefs cook, but never tries it, because he feels he isn't good enough. "I'm going to invite Curly to cook with me. We can make Chicken Cacciatore for my family to enjoy". Chirpy's plan is in motion.

Chirpy sees Curly in math class in school the next day. "Hey Curly! How's it going?" "Hey Chirpy, I'm ok, last night's homework was pretty tough, but I think I got it." "Same here, "Chirpy agrees. "I got kind of stuck on some of the percentages and multiplication," she explains, "but my dad helped me figure it out." Chirpy sits next to Curly. Just before class begins, she asks, "Curly, would you like to go for a bike ride after school?" "That sounds fun!" Curly eagerly answers. "Awesome, let's meet at Lindburgh Field under the big tree behind home plate." "Sounds good Chirpy, is 4 o'clock ok?" Curly asks. "Perfect! See you there." Chirpy feels so hopeful.

As she arrives on her bike, Curly is under the tree. "Wow what a perfect afternoon Curly, let's ride the trail around the park." Off they go on their bikes. "How did you get to be so good at cooking Chirpy?" Curly asks as they pedal. "Well, I learn a lot from my mom and grandmother. I just have a fascination with food, and I watch and help them in the kitchen. I love reading cookbooks too." "That's so cool Chirpy, I wish I could be good at that." he reluctantly admits. "Anyone can cook Curly, it's all about keeping it simple, and having a vision of what you are creating." Chirpy explains. "Would you like to come over and cook with me in my kitchen?" Chirpy asks. "We can make your favorite Chicken Cacciatore with Broccoli." "Sure!" Curly excitedly answers. "Ok, let's talk to our parents and see what night would be good.

Chirpy talks to her mom and she loves the idea. "How about Friday night Chirps?" Mom suggests. "Since you are doing something to help your friend, I'll go to the market and get the ingredients that we can't pick from our garden." "Aw, thank you so much mom." Chirpy hugs her. "I love you mommy." "I love you too kiddo, you're a good friend Chirpy." Chirpy's mom calls Curly's mom, and the plans for Friday night are solidified. Curly is so excited yet a bit scared to go cook with Chirpy.

As Friday night approaches, Chirpy, her mom and dad, and her sisters Jasmine and Ginger are home together. Her brother Derek has a baseball game. They'll leave some food for when he gets home later. Chirpy hears Curly's mom dropping him off outside. "Curly's here!" The doorbell rings and she opens the front door to find Curly dressed so nicely but looking extremely nervous. "Hi Chirpy, these are for your mom." holding an adorable little bouquet of flowers. "How sweet of you Curly, come in." "Hi Curly!" Chirpy's mom comes to greet Curly. "It's so nice to have you over tonight, please make yourself at home." "Hi Mrs. Decorum, thank you so much for having me over, I brought these for you." Curly hands her the flowers. "Oh Curly, they're beautiful, thank you! You are so sweet. They can be the centerpiece on the table with our dinner." "C'mon Curly." Chirpy grabs him, "Let's go start preparing our amazing dinner."

"Tonight, we're cooking Chicken Cacciatore with Rigatoni and Steamed Broccoli." Chirpy has an idea to make Gougeres, a cheesy little baked French pastry, perfect for a quick appetizer. "Let's bake a batch of Pistachio Cookies for dessert Curly! They're so easy and delish." "Gee Chirpy, I have no idea how to make any of those things, I don't want to mess it up." Curly admits. "We're doing this together, here Curly, I have an apron for you to wear while we cook." Chirpy puts it on him and helps him tie it. "Wow Chirpy, I feel like a real chef." "You look like one Curly." Chirpy gets all the ingredients they need for their Chicken Cacciatore. "This takes about an hour to cook, so we'll get this in the oven first. I'll show you how to cut all the vegetables while I start our Cheese Gougeres appetizers, then we'll make the cookies. "This is awesome Chirpy. I'll be careful when I use your knife."

"Ok Curly, Chicken Cacciatore uses chicken thighs and legs, onions, celery, bell peppers, mushrooms, crushed tomatoes and herbs. Tonight, we'll use oregano, thyme, and Italian parsley. We're going to sear the chicken in a pan first, then add the vegetables, tomatoes, then cover it, let it bake until tender and luscious." explains Chirpy. "Let's start with a clean cutting board. Hold the chef's knife firmly and hold the vegetables with your fingers tucked under so you don't cut them instead of the vegetables." Curly starts with the celery, then slowly and carefully cuts all the veggies for their recipe.

Chirpy starts preparing the Gougeres. A simple dough that begins by heating milk and butter in a pot, mixing in flour and salt, then eggs and cheese. Bake them for 25 min in a 400-degree oven. Scrumptious! "We'll bake these in the oven next to the chicken." "How do my vegetables look Chirpy?" "They look great Curly. Our Cacciatore is going to rock. Let's get the chicken seared off." Chirpy takes out a big sauté' pan and heats it. "Chirpy you're so confident with what you're doing." "Practice makes perfect Curly." After they season the chicken with salt and pepper, they add olive oil to the pan, and lay each piece around the pan. "See Curly? You're cooking!" "I am! It smells so good too!" They brown the chicken then add their veggies, the herbs, and crushed tomatoes. "Ok, now it goes in the oven. We can start the Pistachio Cookies." Chirpy grabs the bag of pistachios. "All we do is grind the pistachios in my mom's food processor, mix them with some sugar, honey, vanilla, then egg whites, and we're going to have the most wonderful cookies for dessert." "I'll get the eggs and separate the yolks from the whites." says Curly, feeling increasingly comfortable and confident as they prepare their special dinner.

With the chicken cooking, and the Gougere dough made, they make their pistachio cookies. "Curly check this out, I ground the pistachios, now in this bowl we add some sugar, honey, and egg whites and mix it together." "Can I mix it?" Curly asks, wanting to be involved. "Absolutely Curly, here's my mom's wooden spoon, just mix until it all comes together." Chirpy directs. "Now we scoop them onto this baking sheet and bake them. That's it! In fifteen minutes, these green little jewels will come out of the oven, ready to be dusted with powdered sugar and enjoyed." Chirpy scoops her cheese Gougeres and bakes them. The chicken is just about ready. Let's cook the broccoli and the Rigatoni pasta. We have our pot of boiling water here so drop in the pasta and in 8 minutes, we'll drain it and put it in this bowl with a little olive oil. Just put the broccoli in a pan with a little water and cover it so they steam for 5 minutes.

Chirpy has the picnic table in the backyard set, so they can eat al fresco tonight. "Mom, Dad, Ginger and Jasmine, dinner's ready!" In like 10 seconds, Jasmine appears, "Hey Curly!" She gives him a warm hug. "How impressive, you two made this amazing dinner. The whole house smells like Italy, I can't wait to eat! Thank you for cooking for us." "Your sister did most of it." Curly admits. "Oh no Curly, you did a lot of the cooking and the pistachio cookies." Chirpy insists. "Pistachio cookies?" asks Chirpy's Dad, as he enters the kitchen with Chirpy's mom. "Did you say you made pistachio cookies Curly? Those are my favorite. This all looks awesome!" as he gives Curly a high five. "Curly feels so excited. Ginger notices Cheese Gougeres. "Wait, you made these too? They look so good. Curly and Chirpy, you two are like serious chefs. How cool!" Curly transfers the Cheese Gougeres to a plate. "Everything smells so delicious. Curly young man, you did good." "Thank you, Mrs. Decorum. It was fun and Chirpy's a good teacher. I feel so happy right now to be sharing what we made with you all." Curly feels he has discovered something inside himself that he hasn't really felt before. Being able to share something you made feels pretty darn good. He feels more confident about himself and can't wait to cook this at home for his mom and dad. "I set the picnic table for dinner, so everybody go outside and sit down, Curly and I will bring the food out," Chirpy directs.

With everyone together at the table, they all hold hands. Ginger says grace. "Lord thank you for this beautiful day, this wonderful dinner that Curly and Chirpy cooked and shared with their gifted hands, and their generous spirit. Bless this house, and our mom and dad. Amen."

Cheese Gougeres

Cheese Gougeres are savory, French baked pastries that are delicious, and super easy and cheesy. Perfect appetizers, or a homemade cheesy snack. The dough is started on the stove, then finished off the heat. The French cheese of choice for Gougeres is Gruyere. A quality Cheddar mixed with Parmesan works nicely.

Preheat oven to 400 degrees.

A small 1 oz. scoop or soup spoon will make 20 nice sized Gougeres.

Pate Choux Pastry (Pate Choux means 'hot dough' in French)

- 1 Cup   Water
- 4 oz.   Unsalted Butter (1 stick)
- 1 tsp.   Salt
- ¼ tsp.   Ground Black Pepper
- 1 Cup   A.P. Flour (Sifted)
- 4 ea.   Lg. Eggs
- 2 Cups   Grated Sharp Cheddar Cheese OR Gruyere Cheese
- ½ Cup   Finely Grated Parmesan Cheese

1. In a 3 qt. saucepan, add the water, butter, salt and pepper, bring to a boil.

2. Add the flour and mix together with a wood spoon or rubber spatula. Mix well off the heat until smooth and no lumps.

3. Remove pan from stove, and begin mixing in eggs one at a time, stir together until dough is smooth and eggs are fully mixed in.

4. Stir in all of the cheese until mixed all though the dough.

5. Scoop or spoon each Gougere onto parchment lined baking pan, leave an inch between each one. This recipe makes 20 - 22 pieces.

6. Place in 400 degrees oven for 25 - 30 minutes. Gougeres should be golden brown. Remove from oven, wait a few minutes then enjoy!

Curly's Chicken Cacciatore

A wonderful Sunday afternoon dinner that can be paired with any pasta. Chirpy loves to use mushrooms, carrots, and green peppers in her recipe, but you can add or remove any vegetables of your choice.

Serves 4

Curly's Chicken Cacciatore

- 2 Tbsp.   Olive Oil
- 1 ½ tsp.   Salt
- ½ tsp.   Ground Black Pepper
- 8 pieces   Chicken thighs and legs (Chirpy removes the skin)
- 1 ea.   Sweet Onion
- 2 lg.   Whole Carrots
- 1 lg.   Green Bell Pepper
- 6 oz.   Mushrooms
- 2 ea.   Garlic Cloves (or 1 Tbsp. Minced garlic)
- 2 tsp.   Fresh Rosemary (Chopped
- 1 tsp.   Fresh Thyme leaves (removed from the tiny stems)
- 20 oz.   Crushed Tomatoes
- ½ Cup   Chicken or Vegetable Broth

1. Begin by cutting the vegetables. Peel, then slice the carrots and onions into ¼ inch slices. For the green pepper, remove the top and seeds, then cut into wide strips, then each strip into three pieces. Slice the mushrooms. Chop the garlic into small pieces. Set aside.

2. Season the chicken pieces with salt and pepper.

3. Heat a large saute' pan over medium heat. Add olive oil, then place the chicken into hot pan. You want to brown chicken on both sides, about 15 minutes. Remove the chicken from the pan onto a plate.

4. Add the onions, carrots and peppers back into the pan. Stir around to brown vegetables lightly, about 5 minutes.

(Continue recipe on page 24)

5. Add the mushrooms, garlic, rosemary and thyme. Then add the crushed tomatoes and chicken or vegetable broth. Stir everything together. Taste your sauce, add salt and pepper if desired.

6. Add chicken back into pan, submerging each piece.

7. Bring everything to a boil, turn down to medium low heat, let simmer for an hour uncovered on the stove top. Turn chicken pieces over after 30 minutes to cook thoroughly.

8. When your Chicken Cacciatore is ready. Cook your pasta. In a 4 quart pot, bring 2 ½ quarts of water with 1 Tbsp salt to a boil. Add 12 to 16 oz of your favorite pasta. Follow the pastas cooking directions on the box for how much time to cook it. Chirpy and Curly love Rigatoni with their Cacciatore.

9. While the pasta cooks, remove the chicken from the pan and place each piece in a serving platter with a few spoonfuls of sauce. When the pasta is cooked to your liking, strain it and add it to the rest of the tomato sauce and toss gently. Serve with two pieces of chicken over sauced pasta and enjoy.

Steamed Broccoli with Olive Oil and Lemon

Serves 4

- 2 lg.   Broccoli Crowns
- 3 Tbsp.   Olive Oil
- 2 tsp.   Fresh Lemon Juice
- ½ Cup   Water

1. Wash and cut up the broccoli into individual pieces.

2. Place broccoli into large saucepan with a lid, add ½ Cup water

3. Place pan covered with lid, on stove top, over medium hi heat.

4. When the water boils it will steam the broccoli. Cook for 5 minutes

5. Drain excess water, add olive oil and lemon juice, toss and serve.

Chirpy's Pistachio Cookies

Chirpy's Pistachio Cookies may be the best cookies you will ever taste. Gluten Free, loaded with pistachios, easy and fun recipe.

Pistachio Cookie Dough

- 2 Cups   Toasted Unsalted Pistachios
- ½ Cup   Granulated Sugar
- 1 Tbsp.   Honey
- 1 tsp.   Vanilla Extract
- ½ tsp.   Salt
- 1 ea.   Egg White from Large Egg
- 2 Tbsp.   10X Powdered Sugar

1. Preheat oven to 325 degrees

2. Using a food processor, grind the pistachios and sugar together for about 1 ½ minutes, your nut mixture will look like wet sand.

3. Transfer your pistachios to a bowl, add the honey, vanilla and salt, then mix together with a rubber spatula or spoon.

4. Add the egg white and mix in until you have a moist dough.

5. On a baking sheet with parchment paper, scoop pistachio cookies with a tablespoon sized spoon or 1 oz. Scoop, onto baking sheet. Leave an inch between cookies.

6. Bake cookies for 20 minutes. Cookies should be golden brown and still soft on the inside.

7. Let cool for 15 minutes, then lightly dust cookies with powdered sugar through a sifter to give them a snowy appearance.

Grandpa's Jolly Parisian Jaunt

After hearing about the magic apron, and the hidden powers it may have, Grandpa wants to see it in person. He's curious about what other powers it has. He and Grandma are going to visit Chirpy. It's a breezy Saturday morning in Dazzelton. Chirpy's sitting under her lemon tree Sunny Brighton, doing homework.

"Well good morning young lady." Grandpa says as he gets hugs from Chirpy. "Hi Grandpa, hi Grandma, what a nice surprise. Since your here, how about if I cook for us a nice breakfast?" "That does sound good." Grandma responds, "Actually we haven't eaten yet." Although he's hungry, Grandpa has other ideas at the moment. "Chirpy what do I hear about a Magic Apron? Grandma told me you cooked a dinner with your friend Curly and the apron gave him the power to share." "Grandpa, he like, changed right before my eyes. He was so confident and happy, and I've never seen him like that. I think the Magic Apron helped." Chirpy reflects. "But there may be other powers." Chirpy adds. "Like other magical powers?" Grandpa asks. "Maybe, that's what my friend Madi told me, and she made it." "I have an idea, and I'd like to put the Magic Apron on and see, is that ok Chirpy?" "Of course Grandpa, that's what it's for." Chirpy scurries off to her room to get it.

Returning into the backyard, she opens it to put on Grandpa. "Here, I'll help you tie it." Grandma tells Grandpa "Wow dear, you look kinda cute in that apron," Grandma flirts with Grandpa, "My handsome Chef." Grandpa puts it on. "Wow, I have this incredible feeling going through my body. I've been thinking of something and somewhere I want to go, and wondering if the Magic Apron has the powers to really bring me there." Grandpa reveals his idea. "You want to 'GO' somewhere?"Chirpy excitedly asks, "Like, actually travel?" "Yes!" Grandpa smiles. "Oh boy how cool would THAT be?" Chirpy claps.

Before anyone can say another word, POOF!! Grandpa disappears! Chirpy and Grandma are stunned, they can't believe what just happened. They just look at each other with wide eyes and are shocked. "Grandma? Where's Grandpa?" "Uh, Chirpy, I. Have. No. I. Dea." "Do you think the Magic Apron took Grandpa somewhere? Could that be possible?" Chirpy's in total disbelief. "He was mumbling last night about our honeymoon in Paris, but I don't know what he was talking about." Grandma remembers. "Your honeymoon 50 years ago? Oh boy, this is going to be great!"

Then before they both know it Grandpa reappears with a POP!! "Wait til you two see where I went!" Grandpa exclaims, feeling like he is twenty years younger. "Grandpa where did you go?" Chirpy can't wait to hear. Grandpa turns to Grandma, holds her hand, and says, "Honey, I was transported to Paris back in 1972, when we were on our honeymoon, at the Cafe De L'Amour where we had our favorite dinner. "You did what dear?" Grandma cannot believe her ears. "You were in Paris in 1972, at the place we enjoyed so much on our honeymoon?" She gets a little teary eyed. "Yes. It was awesome." Grandpa hugs Grandma. "I walked around, went into the Cafe and talked with the chef. He said I could come back, and he would have a table for us." "Us?" Grandma responds. "Wait, Grandpa," Chirpy interrupts, "You were only gone for like 10 seconds. How could you have walked around and done all that?" "I don't know Chirpy, but I did." "Us?" Grandma repeats. "What do you mean he has a table for US?" "We are going back there to eat again, just like it was on our honeymoon my love." Grandpa reaches for her hand. Grandma is absolutely overwhelmed with joy. "Can I come?" asks Chirpy, who is so over the moon about what Grandpa just did with the Magic Apron. "Of course, Chirpy, all three of us are going right now." Grandpa insists. "Let's go!! Chirpy responds. "Let's all hold hands and see if it works." Grandma grabs Chirpy's hand, and "POOF"

Before they say another word, they are in Paris 1972, in front of the Palais Garnier, the famous Opera House. "When I was told the Magic Apron has other powers," a mesmerized Chirpy admits, "I had NO IDEA this would be one of them! Grandma, Grandpa, I love you. Can you believe where we are?" Grandma is astonished to be back in the same place, and same year as their honeymoon. "Look dear, there's the Cafe. Just like I remember it." Grandma holds Grandpa tight and whispers in his ear, "You daring rascal, to think of this as a power of that cute little apron. I love it. I can't wait to have the Chocolate Pots de Crème for dessert again!" "Well, let's go to our table." Grandpa leads the way. "Look at this beautiful city." Chirpy cannot believe her eyes. "The cars look so old."

Café de l'amour

Coq au Vin
SOUPE
a l'Oignon
Gratin
Profiterole

"

"Good evening, Madam, Monsieur, Chirpy Gourmet. Welcome. We have a table for three waiting for you." The Maitre d' professionally greets them, "Please follow me this way." "How did you know my name?' Chirpy curiously asks the Maitre d'. He just smiles and winks at her. "Honey it is as beautiful, and the aromas of this amazing food are exactly as I remember it." Grandma whispers to Grandpa. After they sit, they are handed menus, and have their napkins placed in their laps. Chirpy is uber impressed with Grandpa for picking this restaurant on their honeymoon. "This is the fanciest restaurant I have ever seen. It is so beautifully decorated. I can't wait to taste this incredible food!"

After they order, Grandma and Grandpa share stories with Chirpy about their honeymoon. They all order the French Onion Soup, and three steaming, melty crocks soon appear to the table. Each soup overflowing with caramelized melted Gruyere cheese, waiting to be enjoyed to the last drop. They savor every spoonful. The waiters are so meticulous and polite. Next come the entrées. Grandma and Grandpa both ordered the same thing they had on their honeymoon, Chicken Coq au Vin, the classic dish he has been yearning to have again ever since he had it here 50 years ago. Chirpy got so excited and ordered it as well, with a dish of Ratatouille for a vegetable side. The table looks like a magazine photo. The food is perfectly cooked, and every bite is followed by a deeply satisfying "mmmmm."

The dusk turns to night, the city lights brighten the street that is bustling with life. "It's time for dessert!" The moment Chirpy has been waiting for. As the waiter arrives to the table and places their sweet French pastries and confections in front of them, a harmonic "Wooow" fills the air. Chocolate Pots de Crème, a baked chocolate pudding in little pots for Grandpa. Profiteroles, small warm cream puffs filled with vanilla ice cream topped with warm chocolate sauce for Chirpy. A waiter is table side making Grandma Crepes Suzette, freshly made crepes with caramelized sugar, butter, and oranges, then flamed with Grand Marnier, served with vanilla ice cream. Grandma, Grandpa, and Chirpy are all just mesmerized watching this proud, professional waiter making perfect crepes. They all share each other's treats, scraping their forks and spoons to get every bit of sauce on each plate. "That, was amazing." Chirpy sighs. As they all sit back, smile, and laugh at the meal and experience they just had, they POOF! are back in Chirpy's house in the kitchen right where they were Saturday morning. "Grandma, Grandpa, THAT was unbelievable!" "It was, totally unbelievable." Grandma repeats, as she stares at grandpa for thinking of such an incredible adventure to take them on. "We should do it again sometime."

French Onion Soup

This soup can be made vegetarian by using vegetable stock.

Serves 4

- 4 Tbsp.   Olive Oil
- 3 lg.   Sweet Onions (Vidalia or Walla Walla are perfect)
- 5 Cups   Chicken or Beef Stock
- ½ tsp.   Fresh Thyme leaves
- ½ tsp.   Fresh Rosemary leaves (chopped fine)
- 2 tsp.   Worcestershire Sauce
- 2 Tbsp.   A.P. Flour
- ½ tsp   Salt
- ¼ tsp.   Ground Black Pepper
- 4 ea.   Toasted French Bread Slices (about ½ inch thick)
- 2 Cups   Grated Swiss or Gruyere Cheese
- 1 Cup   Shredded Parmesan Cheese

1. Slice the onions into ½ inch thick slices. Set Aside.
2. In a large sauce pot, heat the olive oil on med hi heat. Add onions.
3. Cook the onions until caramelized, about 15 minutes. Stir often.
4. Add the thyme, rosemary, Worcestershire sauce. Then stir in flour.
5. Add the 5 ½ cups broth of your choice, stirring well, bring to a boil.
6. Reduce the heat to medium and cook for 20 - 25 minutes.
7. At this point preheat oven to 400 degrees.
8. Slice your French Bread into ½ inch thick slices. Place on baking dish and toast in oven until golden brown, just 5 or 6 minutes. Set aside.
9. Ladle the soup into 4 crocks, place a crouton in center of each one, sprinkle the Swiss and Parmesan cheeses over each soup, place in the oven to melt cheese. Carefully remove cups from oven and serve.

Chicken Coq Au Vin

This classic French chicken dish is so enjoyable and easy to prepare. It goes perfectly with mashed potatoes. The alcohol burns off during cooking. This recipe cooks on the stove, then finishes in the oven.

4 Servings

- 1 Tbsp.   Olive Oil
- 4 ea.   Chicken Thighs
- 4 ea.   Chickens Legs
- 1/2 Cup   Red Wine   (Pinot Noir, Cabernet work well)
- 2 Cups   Chicken Broth
- 3 ea.   Bacon Strips (Cut into small pieces)
- 1 lg.   Sweet Onion (Sliced into ½ inch slices)
- 4 ea.   Carrots   (Sliced into 1 inch pieces)
- 3 ea.   Garlic Cloves (Chopped into small pieces)
- ½ Cup   Crushed Tomatoes
- 8 oz.   Button Mushrooms, or Crimini (sliced into thick slices)
- 2 tsp.   Thyme Leaves (Remove leaves from stems)
- ½ tsp   Salt
- ¼ tsp.   Ground Black Pepper

1. Preheat oven to 350 degrees.
2. In a large bowl, soak chicken pieces in the red wine for 20 minutes.
3. Cut vegetables and bacon according to instructions above. Set aside.
4. Remove chicken from the wine, saving the wine. Dry chicken with paper towels, and season with salt and pepper.
5. Heat a large ovenproof pan over **medium** heat. Add the bacon and cook about 4 minutes, stirring bacon frequently. Remove bacon from pan.
6. Add chicken to brown each side, about 4 minutes per side. If all the chicken doesn't fit, brown off 4 pieces at a time. Remove chicken from pan.
7. Add the olive oil, then the onions and carrots to cook for 3 minutes.
8. Add the crushed tomatoes, garlic, and bacon. Stir everything together.
9. Add the wine and chicken broth, turn heat up to medium high.
10. Let liquid gently boil for 5 minutes, then stir in the mushrooms and thyme.
11. Add chicken back into pan, submerge into liquid, then bring back to a boil. Place your pan into the oven and bake for 1 hour. The liquid will turn into a luxurious sauce and chicken and vegetables will be moist and tender.

Ratatouille

Kids all over France enjoy their family's Ratatouille. Vegetables from the garden are seared on the stove then baked together to make this wonderfully flavorful and nutritious side dish. Chirpy loves it!

Serves 6 - Preheat oven to 350 degrees.

- 4 Tbsp.   Olive Oil
- 1 ea.   Red Onion - Medium Size
- 1 ea.   Yellow, Red, or Orange Bell Pepper - Large
- 1 ea.   Zucchini - Large
- 1 ea.   Yellow Squash
- 1 ea.   Eggplant - Medium Size
- 3 ea.   Plum Tomatoes
- 3 ea.   Garlic Cloves - Chopped
- ¼ Cup   Crushed Tomatoes
- ¾ tsp.   Oregano - Dried or Fresh
- 7 ea.   Large Basil Leaves
- ½ Cup   Italian Parsley - Chopped
- 1½ tsp.   Salt
- ½ tsp.   Ground Black Pepper

1. Wash then cut all of the vegetables. There is no specific way to cut each vegetable, slices and big 1 inch chunks are all good.

2. Chop the garlic into small pieces. Pull the parsley leaves off the stems to get ½ cup. Chop the Basil into wide slices.

3. In a large ovenproof pan, heat the Olive Oil over medium hi heat.

4. Add the Onions, Peppers, Zucchini, and Yellow Squash and sear for 3 minutes, stir so nothing stick to the pan. Add ½ tsp Salt and Pepper.

5. Add the Eggplant, Plum Tomatoes, and Garlic. Stir together, then add the Crushed Tomatoes, and Herbs. Salt again ½ tsp.

6. Stir everything together to mix the tomatoes and herbs through the vegetables. Place the pan into the oven for 30 minutes.

7. Remove from the oven and enjoy.

Profiteroles and Chocolate Sauce

Profiteroles are so scrumptious! Chirpy loves them the proper French way. Served warm, sandwiched with vanilla ice cream in the middle, and drizzled with warm chocolate sauce. Use your favorite Vanilla Ice Cream.

Makes 24 - 1 oz. Profiteroles

Pate Choux Pastry Puffs

- 1 Cup   Water
- 4 oz.   Unsalted Butter (1 Stick) - slices
- ½ tsp.   Salt
- 1 Cup   A.P. Flour
- 4 ea.   Large Eggs

1. Preheat oven to 400 degrees

2. In a 2 qt. saucepan, add the water, butter, and salt. Bring to a boil.

3. Add the flour and mix with a wood spoon or rubber spatula off the heat until smooth and no lumps. Let dough cool 10 minutes.

4. Begin mixing in eggs one at a time, stir together until dough is smooth and each egg is fully mixed in before adding next egg.

5. Set dough aside. Place a piece of parchment paper on your baking sheet. With a 1 oz. scoop or spoon, scoop dough onto baking sheet about 1 inch apart. Dip the scoop in water between scoops of dough, it will come out onto baking sheet easier.

6. Bake for 30 minutes. Your profiteroles should be a nice golden brown, not lighter in color. Remove from oven and let cool.

7. Serve warm right from the oven. Cut in half like a burger bun, fill bottom with a scoop of vanilla ice cream, place pastry top on ice cream, then drizzle with warm chocolate sauce.

Chocolate Sauce

- 1 Cup   Heavy Cream
- 8 oz.   Semisweet or Bittersweet Chocolate. (Chopped into pieces)

1. Heat heavy cream in a 2 qt. pan until hot. Add chocolate pieces and whisk until smooth. Serve warm over Profiteroles.

Chocolate Pots De Creme

Velvety baked custards so chocolaty delish you'll make this dessert over and over. Add a dollop of whipped cream and you'll be in heaven.

Makes 9 - 4 oz. Servings

Chocolate Custard

- 3 Cups   Half and Half
- ½ Cup   Sugar
- ¼ tsp.   Salt
- 1 tsp.   Vanilla Extract
- 8 oz.   Bittersweet Chocolate (chopped into pieces.)
- 10 ea.   Egg Yolks from 10 Large Eggs

1. Preheat oven to 300 degrees.

2. These custards are baked in their cups, in a water bath to prevent burning. Place 9 - 5 oz. ramekins or glass cups, into a deep sided baking pan. Fill pan around cups with ½ inch of warm water. Set aside.

3. In a 3 qt. sauce pot over medium heat, add the half and half, sugar, salt, and vanilla. Stir and cook until hot, not boiling.

4. Stir in the chopped chocolate, mix until completely melted.

5. In a large mixing bowl, add the yolks and whisk for 20 seconds, then pour the chocolate cream slowly into the yolks mixing constantly.

6. Pour the chocolate custard mix into the empty baking cups, and fill until ½ inch from the top of each cup..

7. Carefully transfer your pan with water and custard filled cups into the oven. Bake 45 minutes to an hour. Your custard should be firm around the edges and slightly jiggly in the middle. Bake longer if needed. Remove cups from baking pan and chill for 45 minutes.

8. Whether topped with whipped cream, berries, chocolate shavings, or as is, you will fall in love with this amazing chocolate dessert.

Crepes Suzette

Golden crepes served in a buttery orange sauce with vanilla ice cream. A French delight that you will love. You can fold chocolate chips, or Nutella, into each crepe to make it even more decadent.

Makes 8 crepes

Crepe Batter

- 1 Cup   Milk
- 2 lg.   Eggs
- ¼ tsp.   Salt
- 1 tsp.   Sugar
- ¾ Cup   A.P. Flour
- 2 Tbsp.   Butter (melted)

1. Combine all ingredients in a blender. Blend until smooth. Set aside.

2. Heat a non stick skillet over medium heat, spray with pan spray, pour in ¼ cup batter and tilt pan to make a round crepe.

3. Cook just until edges are golden brown, flip with a spatula and finish cooking for 20 - 30 seconds. Place crepes on a plate.

Orange Sauce

- ½ Cup   Orange Juice
- 4 Tbsp.   Sugar
- ½ tsp.   Orange Zest
- 3 Tbsp.   Butter
- ¼ tsp.   Salt

1. In the same pan, combine all the sauce ingredients. Stirring often, cook over medium heat, lightly boiling, about 2 minutes. Your orange sauce will have a syrup consistency. Turn heat down.

Serving your Crepes Suzette

1. Fold each crepe in half, then in half again to make triangles. This is where you can add chocolate chips or Nutella inside each crepe. Place each crepe into your warm sauce, coating entire crepes.
2. Serve 2 warm crepes per person, with a scoop of vanilla ice cream.

Lunch in The Big Easy

Last week, Grandpa discovered a hidden power of the Magic Apron and transported Grandma and Chirpy on an unbelievable trip to Paris. Now Chirpy has an idea of her own. She wants to share an experience with her dad. If she could go back in time, surely, she would be able to go somewhere in the present. Chirpy's dad loves everything about New Orleans, the people, culture, and of course the wonderful food. It is heavily influenced by Cajun, Creole, and Soul food. He loves it all, especially the Soul food. Chirpy and her family visited there a few years ago and experienced some of the most delicious cooking in the world. Now she wants to take her dad there for lunch and believes the Magic Apron can take them. He is home today relaxing and reading his new book. This would be a perfect time for them to slip away.

It's close to noon on Saturday and Chirpy just finished her homework. She notices they are the only ones at home, so she brings the Magic Apron downstairs and shares her plans with him. "Hey dad, how's your book?" she asks. "Great reading", he responds, "It's about a boy with dreams of flying." "Dreams can come true if you keep working at it, right daddy?" "Absolutely." Chirpy's spirit always warms his heart.

"It's getting close to lunchtime. Are you hungry Dad?" "Actually, I am" he replies, "I see you're holding your apron, are you planning to cook something Chirps?" "Well, not exactly. How would you like to go have lunch together, like, in New Orleans?" Chirpy dares to ask. "New Orleans for lunch?" he laughs. "That would be so cool. How could we possibly get to New Orleans in time for lunch?" he responds in disbelief. "Wellll, what if I told you I think this Magic Apron could take us there." Dad laughs again, "Really! Well my girl, if you think it can, then I'm all in." "OK, daddy come here." As he puts his book down and gets up from his comfy chair, Chirpy puts the Magic Apron on him, then directs him to stand in front of her. "Hold my hands, close your eyes, and think about where you want to go in New Orleans. Think about the food you want to enjoy." "I can't wait to see what you have up your sleeve Chirpy." as he closes his eyes and thinks of his favorite place.

He starts to feel like he's flying, and then POOF! When he opens his eyes, he sees a man playing saxophone on the corner. They're in Louis Armstrong Park, near the Treme Lafitte section of New Orleans. This is where soul food is king. "Chirpy, we're in New Orleans! How in the world did we get here?" Dad is super perplexed. "It's a hidden power of the Magic Apron, it can transport you to your favorite place." Chirpy begins to tell him the story. "Last week Grandpa and Grandma came over and he took us to Paris with help from the Magic Apron. Today I wanted to take you here because you love it so much." "Are you kidding me?" Dad can't believe what Chirpy is saying. Somehow, they're in New Orleans, and though he's slightly confused, he believes her.

They can hear jazz music being played on the street. Aromas from the wonderful kitchens preparing their delicacies fill the air. "Just being here is making me hungry."Chirpy says with an excited smile. "Me too Chirps. I can't believe we're here." Dad is still in disbelief. "That Magic Apron does have some magical powers." "Let's go find a soul food restaurant," Chirpy suggests, "I know that's your favorite food here." "Sounds great! Let's walk this way." They hold hands as they stroll down Saint Philip St.

Within minutes they meet a couple walking in the same direction. "Hi!" Chirpy greets them. "I'm Chirpy and this is my dad John, he loves Soul Food, can you recommend a place?" "Hello Chirpy and John, nice to meet you, I'm Carter and this is my wife Paisley. We're going to our favorite place, Cafe' Ella May's right now. The owner is our friend. We'd love for you to join us." Carter and John shake hands. "Thank you Carter, very nice to meet you Paisley, we would love to join you." Chirpy and her dad are so excited. "Ella May makes the best fried chicken in New Orleans." Paisley adds. "Chirpy, what a wonderful name, I love your overalls too! Where are you from Chirpy?" "Thank you, Paisley, we live in a small town called Dazzelton." "Well, it must be a Dazzling place." Paisley remarks. "It is," Chirpy responds, "You should come see it sometime." "We may take you up on that one day." The men are chatting as well, mostly about the delicious food that this area is famous for. After they walk for a couple blocks, Carter points to a cute little green house. Out on the sidewalk is a saxophone player swinging along. Chirpy and Paisley start dancing to his grooves, then pull Dad and Carter in to join them. It's moments like this that Chirpy is so grateful for. Being free and connecting with people. "This is Ella May's" Carter tells John and Chirpy, "C'mon, I'll introduce you to her."

As they enter this eclectic restaurant, Ella May, the owner, comes out to greet them. Chirpy and her dad are thrilled to meet such an accomplished chef and business owner. "It's a pleasure to have you here Chirpy and John, no need for menus, I'm sending out my special dishes for you all, including my fried chicken, greens, mac and cheese, candied yams, and cornbread. "That all sounds amazing!" Chirpy's dad exclaims. "Thank you so much Ella May, it's such a pleasure to meet you." "Likewise, John. I hope you're hungry, 'cause I'm cooking up some real good soul food for you today." as Ella May winks at Chirpy. "It smells like heaven in here Ella May, thank you. You have such a beautiful restaurant. We're so blessed to be here with you today."

Carter, Paisley, Chirpy and her dad are all engaged in conversation when a big platter of glorious fried chicken, bowls of green beans, juicy collard greens, sweet yams, mac n cheese, and warm golden corn bread all arrive to the table. "Wow, look at all that food!" Chirpy's so ready for this experience.

"Daddy this is the best fried chicken I've ever tasted, it's so crispy and juicy." "It is. Your mom is not going to believe it when we tell her about this lunch." Dad still wonders how he's going to tell her where they went. "Ella May's greens are my favorite, and her chicken, her green beans, and her corn bread too. I guess it's all my favorite." laughs Carter. Paisley is diving into the yams. "Ella May's done it again." "Thank you so much for your friendship, and for sharing your favorite place with us." Chirpy tells Carter and Paisley. "You raised a lovely young girl, John." "Thank you, Paisley, she sure is." Chirpy leans over and kisses him on the cheek. "You're the best too daddy, I'm so happy we came here together."

As they finish this feast, a big plate of warm beignets, covered with powdered sugar, arrives at the table. "Compliments of Ella May." says the waiter. Beignets are fluffy little doughnuts served all over New Orleans. Ella May's are perfectly sweet and delicious. "The best I've ever had." Paisley expertly claims.

After finishing their lunch, Chirpy takes a few group selfies with Ella May, her dad, Paisley and Carter. "Now we're friends forever. You must come to Dazzelton and I'll cook for us." They exchange cell numbers. "Chirpy, we look forward to that. Friends forever." Paisley hugs Chirpy. As they start walking back toward the park, Chirpy holds her dad's hand and closes her eyes. All of a sudden, POOF! They're back at home in their living room right where they began. "Chirpy, that's some magic apron you have there. What a trip we just took. I can't wait to tell mom when she gets home."

Ella May's Fried Chicken

This recipe is so crispy, juicy and delicious. Using buttermilk to dip the chicken in before frying gives it that extra crispy tenderness.

- 1   Whole Chicken or 8 pieces
- 2 Cups   A.P. Flour
- 2 tsp.   Salt
- 1 tsp.   Black Pepper
- 1 ½ tsp.   Onion Powder
- 1 tsp.   Garlic Powder
- ½ tsp.   Paprika
- ½ Cup   Buttermilk
- 2 qts.   Corn or Peanut Oil (can use vegetable oil of your choice)
- Extra salt and pepper to season the chicken pieces.

1. Heat the oil to 350 degrees in a 4 quart pot or deep iron skillet.

2. Cut the chicken into 8 - 10 pieces, or place pre-cut pieces on a plate.

3. In a large bowl combine the flour, salt, pepper, onion and garlic powders, and paprika. Mix together well with a fork or whisk.

4. Pour the buttermilk into a medium size bowl.

5. Season each piece of chicken lightly with salt and pepper.

6. Dip the pieces of chicken, one at a time, into the seasoned flour, then buttermilk, then back into the flour to coat well.

7. Carefully drop each piece of chicken into the hot oil and fry for 12 to 15 minutes. Fry four pieces at a time to keep oil hot throughout cooking.

8. Place the chicken on paper towels when cooked to soak up excess oil. Serve and enjoy.

Southern Collard Greens

This recipe can be prepared without meat and will still be so delicious!
Simply prepare according to directions without adding meat.

Serves 4 - 6

- 2 Tbsp.   Olive Oil
- 1 Bunch   Collard Greens
- 1 Cup   Vidalia Onion
- 1 Tbsp.   Chopped Garlic
- 4 Cups   Vegetable Stock
- 1 Cup   Smoked Turkey Leg
- ½ tsp.   Salt
- ¼ tsp.   Ground Black Pepper
- 2 Tbsp.   Apple Cider Vinegar

1. Wash the collard greens thoroughly in cold water. To cut, stack several leaves on top of each other, if you want to cut out the stems, cut them off, then roll leaves up from side to side, then tear leaves into different sized pieces.

2. Slice the onion into small rectangle pieces, about 1 inch by ½ inch.

3. Chop the garlic into very small pieces, about 2 cloves

4. If using a whole smoked turkey leg, slice off some of the meat and cut into small chunks until you fill 1 cup. If you like more meat in your collard greens, add more.

5. Heat a 4 qt. sauce pot over a medium flame. Add the olive oil and heat for a few seconds.

6. Add in the onion, cook for 3 minutes stirring often. Add the garlic, then add collard greens. Stir together.

7. Add the vegetable stock, smoked turkey chunks, vinegar, salt and pepper. Stir together, bring heat down to low, cover the collard greens and cook for 1 hour. If you like them more tender, cook for 15 more minutes. Remove from heat and serve.

Big Easy Mac n Cheesy

This recipe can be made with elbow macaroni or shells.
It's Cheesy Weesy Delicously Easy!

Serves 4 as a side dish.

Preheat oven to 375 degrees.

Bread Crumb Topping (Prepare this first)

- 2 Tbsp.   Unsalted Butter
- ½ Cup   Plain Bread Crumbs

1. Melt the butter in small pan over low heat, add the bread crumbs and mix together. Set aside off the heat.

Cheese Sauce

- 3 Tbsp.   Unsalted Butter
- 3 Tbsp   A. P. Flour
- 1 ½ tsp.   Salt
- ¼ tsp.   Ground Black Pepper
- 2 ½ Cups   Whole Milk
- 2 tsp.   Grated Onion
- 3 Cups   Grated Sharp Cheddar Cheese (to melt into sauce)
- 1 Cup   Grated Sharp Cheddar Cheese (to sprinkle on top)
- 10 oz.   Elbow Macaroni or Shells

1. In a 3 qt. pot over medium heat, melt butter and add flour. Stir together to cook. This is a roux, it will thicken the cheese sauce. Cook while stirring to a tan color, about 3 minutes.

2. Stir in the onions and cook 30 seconds. Slowly stir in the milk, then cook until bubbling and thickened, about 4 minutes.

3. Add the cheddar cheese and stir until melted into the sauce. Add salt and pepper to your taste. Turn off heat.

4. In another 3 qt. pot, bring 2 quarts of water to a boil. Add macaroni and cook for 10 minutes, drain, then add to cheese sauce and fold together. Pour everything into a baking dish, cover with extra 1 cup of cheddar cheese, then sprinkle the bread crumbs on top and bake in 375 degree oven for 10 - 15 minutes. Let your Mac N Cheese cool for 5 minutes before eating.

New Orleans Beignets

Makes 30 - 34 Beignets

- ½ Cup   Warm Water
- ¼ Cup   Granulated Sugar
- 1 ½ tsp.   Active Dry Yeast
- 1 lg.   Egg
- 1/3 Cup   Evaporated Milk
- ½ tsp.   Vanilla Extract
- 2 ¾ Cups   Bread Flour
- ¾ tsp.   Salt
- 2 Tbsp.   Unsalted Butter (room temp.)
- 4 Cups   Peanut or Vegetable Oil
- 1 ½ Cups   Powdered Sugar
- ½ Cup   Extra Flour to roll Beignet dough out

1. In a mixing bowl, combine warm water, sugar, and yeast. Stir together and let sit for 15 minutes to activate yeast.

2. Add the egg, evaporated milk, and vanilla. Mix together with a fork.

3. Using the paddle attachment on the mixer, add the flour and salt to the wet ingredients, then mix on low speed until you see a dough form, about 30 seconds. Turn to medium speed and add the soft butter, mix until combined, and dough has a smooth texture. Remove paddle, then bowl from mixer, and cover bowl with a towel to rise for 1 ½ hours.

4. When dough is ready to roll out, heat your oil to 350 degrees in a 10 inch pan or pot. You want oil to be about 2 inches deep.

5. Remove dough from bowl onto a floured surface, and with a rolling pin or with floured fingers, roll or press the dough out to ¼ inch thick rectangle piece. Cut dough into 2 inch squares. They don't have to be perfect. You'll have some odd shaped Beignets. It's all about having fun!

6. Have a cutting board ready with paper towels on top, to put your Beignets on after frying, and a slotted spoon to remove Beignets from oil. Fry about 5 - 6 at a time, placing them in the oil VERY CAREFULLY. Fry them about 45 seconds on each side, turning them a couple times during frying so they brown evenly. Frying for a total of 3 minutes. Check them by cutting one in half.

7. Once Beignets are fried, sift powdered sugar over each one. Enjoy!

Recipe Index

About The Author

Robert Bellini is an Author and professional Pastry Chef. He is a graduate of the Culinary Institute of America. Ever since he was a young boy, Robert has had a passion for cooking and fresh food. Culinary arts have always come naturally to him. He loves to learn about different cultures through food and cooking. Being in the kitchen with loved ones, sparking feelings, connections, and memories that last forever, have always been an important part of Robert's life. The most gratifying moments are when he gets to share his creations with family and friends.

Robert's affection and respect for photography have led him to study that artistic medium throughout his adult life. Writing has always been a creative outlet as well. He has been told countless times, "You have quite the imagination!" Chirpy was created to bring that youthful imagination to life in stories that people of all ages can enjoy. Besides creating and writing the stories, he does all of the cooking, baking, food styling, and photography for Chirpy Gourmet and Chirpy's Tasty Adventures Kid's Cookbook Series.

He created Chirpy Gourmet to fulfill his dream of bringing families around the world together through reading and cooking.

Contact Robert@Chirpygourmet.com

NOTES